Love's Solace

Poetry of the Soul

NICOLA MARIA LYTLE

THE CHOIR PRESS

First published in the United Kingdom in 2019 by
The Choir Press

ISBN 978-1-78963-037-4

Dedication

For you dearest mum;
Always in my heart.

'I wish for you
The solace
And joy
Of knowing
The timelessness of your love,
And being loved.'

Linda Lytle

Contents

Naomi Lytle

Within the Arms of Grace

Another year
Of trying to reach and love you
With this most unwelcome language.

What if
We could learn to love this new tongue;
Could learn
To keep listening and looking
With ears, and eyes
And above all
Heart wide open,
To this fresh language
Of love between us?

Perhaps if yielded to
With bravery
And wholeheartedness
It holds its own strange beauty –

Beyond form,
Beyond time,
Within the arms of grace.

എൻൿ

Swallows

Enough
Of these sorrows,
Spoke out my heart;

They have been many
And they have been weighty,

And the gap between them
Brief.

They are part of me
But they are not me.

And then appeared a magpie,
Flash of turquoise
Between the sun and the branch;

Just the one for sorrow.

A shower of griefs
Rains down
Rains down.

My heart cracks open
Wider
To contain this new,
Unwelcome sorrow.

A flight of swallows
Takes to the sky

Towards a horizon, steeped
In grace.

⊙⌒◇⌒⊙

Shapeshifter

That inimitable twinkle
As you said:
"I think I'd get bored
On the other side,
So I'd probably send
Mischievous signs
To those I love."

Carefree belly laughs
Connected us
Like an umbilical cord,
One to the other.

I wish I felt like laughing now.

Though you would probably
Prod me to,
For the sheer synchronicity of it.

Instead
Your absence
Finds its presence
In new and varied ways,

And it weighs –
It weighs,
Shapeshifter
On my soul
And my life,

And I wait,
I wait
For your signs of love,
Which I sense
Are more vibrant
Than that burnished orange
Of yours,
Draped around benevolent Buddhas worldwide,
And which I know
Soar
As high, higher
Than those peak experiences
That we spoke of,
And high above
The steadfast mountain peaks
Of your majestic Isle of Skye.

Oh but I miss you.

Drops of Grace

There was a before
And this is the after.

Perhaps the biggest part of me
Is still inhabiting the before;
The space where
The full force of your presence
Beamed into my daily life
Through the apertures
Of these fragile human senses –
Of sight
And sound
And scent
And touch.

And now
Now, you come to me
Are with me
And are me
In a myriad of creative ways
Which overwhelm
And delight
And astound me.

Laced with the missing,
And the aching
They nevertheless
Are drops
Of comfort
And of grace.

༄

Linda Lytle

River of Peace

A river of peace
Flows
Just beyond
The edge of this pain.

It aches to wrap itself
Around your suffering;

It beckons you
To abandon yourself to it
With a fierce child-like trust,
And a bliss-filled gratitude.

This river has a name –
It is your soul.

❦

Eva May (always known as May) Robinson

Red is the Colour

Red is the colour
Of my love for my mother
And of my mother's love for me;

Bursting through
The greyness of my grief,

Warming
The bitter chill
Of my battered heart,

Breathing
Joy and life
And love-
Triumphant,
Back into
This forlorn landscape
Of motherlessness.

Red is the colour
Of my love for my mother
And of my mother's love for me.

❦

Naomi Lytle

Fragments

Fragments of you
Already flash at me,
Both vivid and
Receding
And heartbreakingly
Tender in their ordinariness.

༄

Heavenly Kisses

What if
These bursts of colour,
These sparks of joy
And ribbons of peace,

Are you–

Winking and waving
At us,

And blowing us your
Heavenly kisses?

ര∽ை

Silence Sings

I have passed through
The season of raw grieving;
The season where there had to be
In equal intensity
Flashes of light, dazzling
And the soft sound
Of falling feathers
And grace.

This is the season
Of the aching absence,
Expansive,
Where I look, and I ask
And I listen,
And the silence
Sings back to me.

လ⌒⌒ၜ

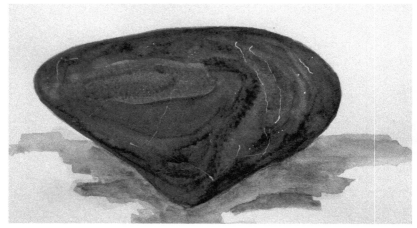

Linda Lytle

Anchor

My heart
Closed itself, clam-like
In readiness
For its next
Brutal severing
Away from
Another tie
To the closeness of you;
From yet another anchor
To the shape and colour of your love.

But in crept
Through the tiniest crevice,
And in the darkest darkness
Of night,
Your loving nudge –
Insistent, as in life,
Carrying your flame of devotion –
And my heart reopened;
Sweet with relief
And with the knowledge
Of your ever-present love
As the sole true anchor.

♥

Boxing Day Birds

Stillness in
The silver sky

Our trees are alive
With you

Teeming

Boxing Day Birds
Making the most of
The hiatus

To sing with sheer delight
Just for the sake of it.

I have my very own birds
Fluttering and boxing
For airspace.

രുക്കുരു

Shade and Shape of Love

And today
I feel
Every day
We are called
To give
A particular shade
And shape
Of love;

Never
With the same chance
Again.

Will we listen
To the call?

Will we give
What has been given
To us
To give?

❦

Linda Lytle

To Dance

To dance
Is
To say yes

To dance
Is
To smile into my heart

To dance
Is
To remember
The joy of you in my
Bones

To dance
Is
To sing this body
Back into life

To dance
Is
To be glad again
To be alive.

ᙣᙏᙎᙏ

Spaces of Softness

It's in moments of beauty
That I find you,

In spaces of softness
That I feel you,

And in the tender ache
Of kindness
That I know you.

❦

Linda Lytle

(Copied from an original painting by Edward Hopper)

A Luminosity so Fierce

An impulse towards the light
I could barely comprehend at first;
For it seized hold
Of something more primal
Than the dry husk of my understanding.

An impulse towards the light –
For the corners of my mouth
Had been parched
For too long now,
And my soul knew
It had a different song to sing.

An impulse towards the light –
A luminosity so fierce
I had to either turn away,
Back to the safety
Of hibernation,
Or dive into it
And die to my safety;
But be changed
And more alive
From this moment on.

❦

Bridge of Love

I see you
Hear you, feel you –
There is hardly a corner
Where I do not find you.

And when the veil is too dense,
I look to our cuckoos to pierce it
With the sound of their persistent calls.

I wish for you
The solace
And joy
Of knowing
The timelessness of your love,
And being loved –
Right where you are,
Right where we are,

And on the bridge between the two you sung of,
And our cuckoos sing of –

On our bridge of love.

❧

What If

What if
We have just one shot
To show who we are,
Who we truly are;

To stop
The forgetting,
The terminal amnesia.

To grab hold
Of the tail coats
Of each day;
To display

Our magnificence?

❦

Linda Lytle

Bejewelled

I hold you
In my hand,
Compact and brimming
With tales of love, and
Loss and longing –
But mainly
Sudden apparitions of
Love and light
And immense comfort.

I hold you
In my eyes,
Bejewelled,
Glinting
And hinting
Of untold treasures.

I hold you
In my heart;
The deepest, richest
Treasure trove
Of all.

If I had to paint
A colour,

I would paint
Your pillar-box red.

In Time

Time to remember
Who you are again,

And in between
And today, what shall you say?

How will your hands touch
This world?

What vibrations
Will you voice from within?

From a distance
We are instruments;

In time
We will look back upon this,
And smile.

౿ಌஐ

The Cycle of Life

That call
At that particular time
Had the familiar sound
Of dread.

But this time
Dread wasn't calling.

Instead –
The ring of your voice
Chimed
The sound of hope
And sweet mercy
To penetrate
My heart.

The cycle of life
Turns,
And life gives you back to me
In beauty-drenched
Creative ways.

Perhaps life
Never really took you away
In the first place.

☙❧

Naomi Lytle

Final Blush Breath

Tree top
Branches
Dipped
In the pink
Light,
Swaying
In this final
Blush breath
Of winter sun.

❧

'Is it so small a thing
To have enjoy'd the sun,
To have lived light in the spring,
To have loved,
To have thought,
To have done.'

Matthew Arnold

❦

Personal Note

I feel incredibly blessed to have received such generous expressions of love and support from my family, friends and mentors along the way. I would like to say a huge thank you to each and every one of you – you know who you are!

I would like to say a particularly heartfelt thank you to my inspirational mum and dad for your unconditional love for me and belief in me.

I would like to say a special thank you to my talented and big-hearted sister for your collection of stunning works of art and your loving encouragement.

I would also like to thank my awesome nephew, Hugo. You are a constant source of pride and joy to me.

Lastly, I would like to say a big thank you to everyone at The Choir Press for your patience, good humour and expertise.

With love and gratitude

Nicola

lovessolacepoetry@gmail.com

'Goodbyes are only for those who love with their eyes
because for those who love with heart and soul,
there is no separation.'

Rumi

Linda Lytle

Paintings and artwork by my mother, Linda Lytle, sister,
Naomi Lytle and nan, Eva May Robinson,
with deep gratitude.

Cover design created by Naomi Lytle

Lightning Source UK Ltd.
Milton Keynes UK
UKHW020828280919
350584UK00008B/52/P

9 781789 630374